MW01194428

Healing Past the Hurt:

My Journey of Recovery, Healing, and Resilience

Healing Past the Hurt:

My Journey of Recovery, Healing, and Resilience

Stephanie Mitchell

Copyright © 2023 **by Stephanie Mitchell**

ISBN: Softcover   978-1-941574-23-2

All rights reserved. No part of this book may be reproduced or transmitted in any form or by any means, electronic or mechanical, including photocopying, recording, or by any information storage and retrieval system, without permission in writing from the copyright owner.

Unless otherwise noted, all scriptures are from THE HOLY BIBLE, ENGLISH STANDARD VERSION®, Copyright© 2001 by Crossway, a publishing ministry of Good News Publishers. Used with permission.

Contents and/or cover may not be reproduced or transmitted in whole or in part in any form or by any means electronic or mechanical, including photocopying, recording, or by any information storage and retrieval system without the express written consent of the publisher.

This book was printed in the United States of America.

To order additional copies of this book, contact:
authorstephanie2023@gmail.com

DEDICATION

I dedicate this book to my mom, Angeline Mitchell, and to my firstborn son, Anthony Walker. They both have blessed my life tremendously. May both of them rest in peace! This book is also dedicated to the people whose lives will be transformed while reading this book.

ACKNOWLEDGEMENTS

I would like to thank my heavenly Father who is the head of my life. Without Him, I would not have made it through it! I thank Him for keeping me through it all and strengthening me to keep going.

I give special thanks to Legacy Center Church for walking me through inner healing and deliverance and welcoming me with open arms as a member.

Thank you to Timothy Lane for walking me through deliverance and grief counseling. It made a huge difference in my life.

I would like to thank Cindy Jumat for my healing journey through grief counseling. My life will be forever changed.

I would be remiss if I did not give special thanks to my family and circle of friends for being there during the losses and for always giving support and love through good times and tough times. I am more than grateful for your prayers and standing in the gap for me.

I appreciate each and every one of you.

May God continually bless you all.

TABLE OF CONTENTS

Foreword   8

Introduction   9

Chapter 1: The Little Girl   10

Chapter 2: Sweet Sixteen   18

Chapter 3: Jumping from the Pan into the Fire   26

Chapter 4: A Different Lifestyle   34

Chapter 5: Making a U-turn   42

Chapter 6; My Last Monday   49

Chapter 7: Loss of My Mom   58

Chapter 8: Release and Be Free   67

ABOUT THE AUTHOR   76

FOREWARD

Stephanie is an amazing woman of God, mother, sister, and friend. I have known her for over twenty years. In those years, I have been there to experience the tremendous growth in her life. Through all those years, her humility has never changed. Over the last few years, I've seen her hunger for the things of God and chase after the things of God like a trailblazer! Her growth is amazing. I believe her ministry and faith has given her new life.

God has given her so much boldness because she knows she is protected by Him. She speaks her truth, life experiences, the hurt, the pain, the forgiveness, and healing in her story. I cannot even begin to tell you all the amazing things about this woman; that would be a book within itself. But as you read her story, I pray that it touches your life in a way you never have experienced before, and I know as you read these pages, you will discover that it was God working in her life throughout the years. As I always say there is "purpose in our pain." Let God heal you, so you can help the next person who needs you!

Let this book be a tool to guide you in not only receiving your own healing but also let it be an instrument to help you facilitate and aid in the healing of others.

Kim J Maryland, Relationship Coach/MFT

INTRODUCTION

"And we know that for those who love God all things work together for good, for those who are called according to his purpose" (Romans 8:28, ESV).

There is purpose in our pain. Everything we go through has a purpose. God can take a broken thing and make it beautiful. He said He will give us beauty from ashes. Isaiah 61:3 says, "And provides for those who grieve in Zion, to bestow on them a crown of beauty instead of ashes, the oil of joy instead of mourning, and a garment of praise instead of a spirit of despair. They will be called oaks of righteousness, a planting of the Lord for the display of his splendor."

Trauma, if not dealt with, can hinder you in so many ways. Suffering through traumatic experiences or just trying to survive them may destroy you if you are not seeking healing. This book will walk you through my journey of trauma and the issues that I faced because of it. My desire is to let people know that trauma is not the end. Trauma needs to be healed, and it is okay to seek help.

No matter where you find yourself on your road to recovery and healing, always recognize that God restores. It does not matter how slow the process is, your life can be transformed. Trust God enough to open your heart and let Him come in, even into your secret places, and watch "soul remodeling" take place.

Chapter 1:

The Little Girl

Looking back over my life, I think about all that I have endured. As a child, the quiet little girl felt alone and like she could not talk to anyone. I came from a family that did not give hugs or always say I love you. I knew my parents loved me; they just did not always say it. My mom and dad separated when I was about seven years old. I remember moving to Maryland to stay with my aunt, my mom's sister, after the separation. We lived with her for several years until my mom got her own apartment. We were so excited to get our own apartment. She enrolled us in our new school, and we made new friends in our new neighborhood.

My mom and dad got a divorce. I was angry but never told my mom how I felt. She told us that my dad was about to get married again. I felt like he abandoned us, and he left us to be with another family. We finally got to meet our stepmom and our stepsister. They were nice, but I still did not understand why he could not be with my mom and our family. As time went on, I began to love my stepmom and my stepsister. She was so nice to us and treated us like we were her kids. She never treated us differently.

When I was about ten, my mom put a Dark and Lovely relaxer in my hair, and my hair was damaged so badly that she had to cut it really short. I had to get a Jheri curl, so my hair could grow back. I hated that curl. I did not even want to go to school anymore because of it. I really started to hate myself, and I looked in the mirror and thought I was ugly.

My siblings and I went to church every Sunday with my great aunt. She picked us up, and we stayed in church all day. I liked going to church but not being there all day. My aunt made me sing in the choir. I sang and cried at the same time because I did not want to do it.

A relative from North Carolina came to stay with us for the summer. She always slept on the couch. Her boyfriend came over to stay with her a few nights. One night, my mom was either working or gone out, and our visitor was asleep. Her boyfriend came into my room while I was asleep and put his hands in my underwear. I woke up, but I pretended to be asleep. I was so terrified. He did it several times when he visited. If he heard my relative move or wake up, he would run out of the room and come back when she went back to sleep. I was so scared that he would hurt me. I went into my brother's room and tried to wake him up, but he was sleeping soundly. So, I went back to bed and went back to sleep. The next morning, I did not tell my mom or my relative because I was afraid.

My cousin came to stay with us for a while after that happened. She came up for summer break. We are the same age. She is two years older than me. My relative's boyfriend tried the same thing against her. The next day, she told her mom. My relative and my mom questioned both of us, and then I explained what he had done. She broke up with him immediately. We never saw him again. That was the first time a man touched me. The second time was when I was about eleven. It was a family member who bribed me with all kinds of stuff to get in bed with him without any clothes on. He always got on top of me and humped. But he never penetrated me. This went on sometimes when I visited. I never told anyone, not even my mom or my dad. I knew that if I told my dad he would kill him.

I was always quiet and did not talk much. After a while, I began to hate myself even more. I took it out on my sister by being mean to her, teasing her, and calling her names. My mom spanked me many times for doing that. I got in trouble a lot for breaking her toys and treating her badly. There was also a time when I was younger and one of my relative's husbands almost made an advance toward me. I stayed with that relative one

Stephanie Mitchell

weekend, and her husband would ride the kids out for a while. That particular day, I was the only one that went with him. While we were riding down the road, he asked me if he could put his hands in my pants. I told him no. I was frightened immediately. After that, I was extremely uncomfortable around him. When I got home, I told one of my siblings. I found out after telling her that he had tried something with her too. We went and talked to an adult in my family. She took us to that relative's house to question her and him about it. He was not home. My relative asked what was wrong. When we told her what happened, she said that we were lying about him. She even convinced my other family members that we were lying. After that, we never mentioned it again.

My mom and I had a conversation after I became an adult about sexual abuse. She told me about a time when I was fourteen, and she had a boyfriend who stayed with us. During our conversation, she told me that he paid more attention to me than he did her. As a result, she had to get rid of him because eventually he would try something. She saw it beforehand and put a stop to it before it happened. At that time, I still never shared with her my experiences. I just did not know how. I did not know how she would react or if she would blame herself, and I did not want her to do that.

You have to be incredibly careful who you leave your children with. I never told them because I was afraid. I was never threatened or anything but just afraid. Children are not always going to tell. I think as adults and parents, we have to ask. We have to sit our children down and let them know that they can talk to us about anything no matter how embarrassing it may feel. I think we have to make them comfortable enough to come to us with anything. Sometimes people can trick children and have them thinking that it is okay. They may say things like, "It's our little secret."

Around the age of fourteen, I used to get picked on because I was quiet. When I came home from school, this girl always followed me and my brother home. My brother was younger than I was. She picked a fight with me every day. I just kept walking. One day, she followed us home, and my brother took up for me while she was picking a fight. The next time she picked a fight, he was not there, but I finally stood up to her. I never had a problem with her again. We became really good friends.

As time went on, as a result of what I had been through, I became promiscuous. The very first guy that I was with took my virginity and never spoke to me again. I was hurt. My friends and I started hanging out more. We then tried a drug called love boat. I cannot even remember where we got it from, but we smoked it. After smoking it, I walked around the neighborhood crying for no reason.

We were young and wanted to do what other people were doing. I sneaked in and out of my bedroom window. My mom thought I was sleeping, but I was out with my friends at night. We went to parties or simply hung out. Then, I started sleeping with a childhood friend. I sneaked him in and out of my bedroom window sometimes, so we could have sex. I was ashamed of my body. Even though he told me I had a beautiful body, I did not think so. I hated my body and always covered myself up, and I did not want guys to see me with my clothes off.

Later, I entered into a relationship with an older guy. My mom found out that I was having sex and put me on birth control pills at fifteen. Around that time, we were unaware that my mom was using drugs. We just knew we kept a lot of company. They were coming over every day. Her boyfriend was the one who introduced her to the drugs.

I spent a lot of time with my childhood friends. I often spent the night at my friend's house. Even though my mom was using drugs at the time, we never went without anything. We always had clothes, shoes, furniture, food, and everything we needed. She also kept up with our doctor appointments, and she made sure we went to church every Sunday. We could not miss one Sunday. Our house eventually got raided by the police. My siblings and I did not really understand what was going on. My mom was taken by the police, and my dad came to Maryland to get us. I did not want to move to North Carolina. I was fifteen, so I decided to stay with my uncle and my cousin in Maryland.

My family was separated; my mom went to prison for two years, and my sister and brothers moved to North Carolina with our dad. I was so hurt. I continued to go to school every day, but sometimes I broke down in class because of everything that happened. My teacher sent me to the guidance counselor because of it. It was hard for me to stay focused in school. My uncle made sure that I had everything I needed. He was my mom's brother, and he treated me like I was his daughter. Even though my mom was only gone for two years, it seemed longer. I could only communicate with her when she called. That was an extremely hard journey for me, especially because I was a teenager who really needed her mom.

REFLECTIONS

I kept secrets when I was a child because I was afraid and did not know how to explain certain things to my mom, and I did not want her to blame herself. Have you ever kept secrets? If so, what, and why?

_____

_____

_____

_____

_____

_____

_____

_____

_____

_____

_____

_____

Have you ever found yourself doing things you should not just to be like everyone else? What did you do? How did it make you feel? This can be either as a child, teenager, or as an adult.

_____

_____

_____

_____

_____

_____

_____

_____

_____

_____

_____

Chapter 2:
Sweet Sixteen

"He took our infirmities and bore our diseases" (Matthew 8:17b, ESV).

At sixteen, my mom was still incarcerated, and I still lived with my uncle in Maryland. One of my cousins was living there with her dad also. We were remarkably close. I was only a couple of years older than her. She was like a sister to me. I missed my mom so much, so I decided to move back to North Carolina with my dad, stepmom, and siblings. They enrolled me in school. Once I started school, I met some new people, connected with some cousins who were my age, and built relationships with them. I visited my cousins' house sometimes on the weekends. I met a lot of new people through them.

Everybody always talked about my accent. They loved it. I guess being raised in Maryland since I was a little girl, my accent was what people called "proper." I started doing my own hair and then started doing my friends' hair also. I made enough money to buy my own school clothes. I styled hair out of my dad's home at that time. I became really close friends with a young lady whose hair I did. I met her through another friend. She started introducing me to her family. We found out later that we were cousins.

I had a grandfather that I had never met. She was very close with him, so she told him about me. He was my mom's dad. My mom never talked to us much about him. They did not have any communication. So, he reached out to me and my siblings and invited us over to his house for dinner. I was glad just to have met my granddad for the first time. After that, we stayed connected until his passing.

As time went by, I tried to get through my last years of school. Most sixteen-year-olds go to school dances, play games, and prepare for junior prom. Unfortunately, I did not do any of those things during my junior year. I had just relocated, leaving everything that I was familiar with for something new. I was accustomed to spending the summer with my dad or grandmother but not staying full-time. It was a big change in my life. Having to move in with my dad and stepmom for good was complicated because of the living arrangements.

It was my dad, stepmom, her daughter, my sister, and my two younger brothers. My dad and my stepmother always made sure we had everything we needed. I did not like that I had to leave all my childhood friends from Maryland. We were close. I missed the friendships I built with them. It hurt knowing that I may not ever see them again. I did not like having to learn about new people, teachers, and my way around a new school. I was always shy and was not good at making new friends. So, it was incredibly challenging for me. I had two cousins that were at my school, so I was able to hang out with them sometimes. But I finally started adjusting to the change. I actually liked North Carolina.

After being in North Carolina for a while, my body started to go through some changes. I did not know why or understand what was going on. I noticed that my urine started to turn dark orange. Everybody else noticed that my eyes started turning yellow. I do not recall feeling bad or being in any pain. We did not know why or what was going on.

My stepmom and dad took me to the doctor. The doctor ran tests, trying to find out what was wrong with me. Several doctors and nurses came by and looked at me. They even walked by the room and stared at me. The way they stared at me made me nervous and uncomfortable. I did not know what was going on. I really got scared after they stared at me. They ran test after test, and I got poked with needles so much that I was tired.

Stephanie Mitchell

When my test results came back, I tested positive for hepatitis. Hepatitis is a general term that means inflammation of the liver. Viral infections are the most common cause of hepatitis. Of course, at sixteen, I had no idea what that was. My stepmom and dad did not even know what it was. I think at that time, hepatitis was very rare. I do not think they saw a lot of cases of it. I think that is why they were staring.

They explained everything to my dad and stepmother. A different virus is responsible for each type of viral hepatitis. Hepatitis has five main viral classifications. They are hepatitis A, B, C, D, or E. They did not know which one mine was. Type A and E can be contracted through food, water, and close contact, and that makes it highly contagious, so they had me quarantined until they knew for sure what type I had. I could not be around my family at all. I could not go to school. My siblings came to my bedroom window to communicate with me. My friends came to my bedroom window to see me or talk with me also. They asked what was wrong with me, but I could not tell them. They could see my eyes were yellow, so they knew something was wrong.
My family put my food at the door. I felt so alone. I still did not understand it. I could not be around anyone until they called, or we got the rest of the information about the virus. I cannot quite remember how long I had to be quarantined, but it seemed like forever. Sitting in a room all alone day after day made me lonely. I was grateful that my siblings and family checked on me from time to time and for my friends coming to do a window visit to keep me company.

Well, results came back, and I had hepatitis B. Hepatitis B is a vaccine preventable liver infection caused by the hepatitis B virus (HBV).

Hepatitis B is spread when blood, semen, or other bodily fluids from a person infected with the virus enters the body of someone who is not infected. It can be spread through sexual contact, sharing needles, syringes, or other drug injection equipment, or from mother to baby at birth. We believed mine was contracted through sex with the guy I was in a relationship with when I stayed in Maryland. He was older than me. My stepmom told me to reach out to him to let him know, but I no longer had his number. We had broken up before I moved in with my uncle.

When I found out I had it, I was so afraid because I did not know what it was or if it would hurt me. At sixteen, I had never even heard of this infection and not knowing what to expect was devastating. All those trips back and forth to the doctor getting treatments exhausted me. The Lord was gracious enough to heal me from the infection. I am truly blessed that it did not affect my liver in any way. They had to keep an eye on my liver functions. It could have been a lot worse. The infection could cause the liver to be inflamed. My liver could have gone into liver failure, and I could have needed a transplant. I know that there are people who have it and never recover. I personally know someone who had hepatitis and passed away. I am forever grateful that God saw fit to heal me.

God is my healer and my restorer. In the midst of everything, His hands were upon my life. He always has the last say. I am so grateful for the healing and restoration. I was young and did not know anything about the sickness. I did not know what to expect. I really did not know God fully at that time in my life either. I just knew there was a God but never had a godly encounter.

I know that God kept me for a reason. He let me live for a reason, and I will not be ashamed to share what I went through. We overcome with the blood of the Lamb and by the word of our testimony. So, my testimony can help someone else share their story and not be ashamed. God will get all the glory. Isaiah 53:5 says, "But he was wounded for our transgressions, he was bruised for our iniquities: the chastisement of our peace was upon him; and with his stripes we are healed."

Stephanie Mitchell

So whatever sickness or disease you may be dealing with, just know that God will carry you through it. He will heal and restore you. Do not give up hope. Do not give up. Keep the faith. The Lord said we only need faith the size of a mustard seed. Continue to pray. Continue to seek Him. Continue to stay in His presence. Continue to speak life and speak His promises back to Him. Find scriptures on healing to read and speak over yourself. I encourage you to pray to God and ask Him to show you someone who you can trust to walk with you during your process. You do not need to do it alone. I was young when I was sick, but now I know how to declare God's word over my life. He is so faithful to His word. He said He will never leave you or forsake you. Even in the midst of our sickness or struggle, He is always right by our side. He will strengthen us through it all.

REFLECTIONS

God healed me from hepatitis. Has He healed you from anything? If so, what?

_____
_____
_____
_____
_____
_____
_____
_____
_____
_____
_____
_____

Do you have mustard seed faith? We can demonstrate our faith by not becoming doubtful of God's word. How do you demonstrate your faith?

_____
_____
_____
_____
_____
_____
_____
_____
_____
_____
_____
_____

What are you believing our faithful God to do for you today?

_____
_____
_____

_____

_____

_____

_____

_____

_____

_____

_____

_____

_____

Chapter 3:

Jumping from the Pan into the Fire

I walked down the street one day in my old neighborhood. A guy drove up in a gray Nissan Sentra with rims and tinted windows. His window was rolled down. The music was booming and sounded good. I really checked him out. He asked for my number, and I gave it to him. He did not call right away but called some days later. We talked for a while on the phone. Then we started dating. By then, he had a Jeep Tracker. He was one of the first guys in the hood to get a Tracker. I really dug him. He started picking me up, and we rode out and spent lots of time together. Then we fell in love.

He was one of the drug dealers in Rocky Mount. I did not know that in the beginning, but I knew he had wonderful things. Even after I discovered he was dealing drugs, I stayed in the relationship and ended up moving in with him. I was seventeen years old at the time and still in school. I tried to get up and go to school like I was supposed to, but there were times when he would turn my alarm off after I fell asleep. He bought all of my school clothes and everything I needed for school during this time.

We found out I was pregnant by him. He took me to Maryland to meet his mom. She told me to get rid of my baby because he was not going to take care of it. Of course, I did not take her advice. I was living my best life. I had jewelry, clothes, shoes, plenty of money, and kept my hair done. We took pictures together wearing our matching outfits. That was the thing back then, to dress alike and take professional pictures. He also rented cars for me to drive around in. He taught me how to drive, but I did not have a license at the time.

I was so in love or so I thought. I really loved the fact that he took care of me. At that time, it was just him and me at home. Then things changed. When I got further along in my pregnancy, he became abusive. He started hitting and choking me. He beat me and dragged me by my hair one day. Then he took me home, and I laid in the bed scared because I did not feel my baby moving for the rest of the night. I cannot quite remember why he did that. Normally, it was because of an argument or because I was not in place, and he could not reach me. I never did anything to him for him to beat me. After beating me, he acted like nothing happened. That was the first time. It happened a couple times during my pregnancy.

After my son was born, the beatings continued. Sometimes, he just choked me. One day, he choked me until I almost lost consciousness. He was very jealous and controlling and did not want me to go anywhere or have many friends. He did not want anyone getting close to me and even kept me isolated from my family sometimes. We spent a lot of time staying in hotels.

He never cared about hitting me in public or in front of his friends. He had only one friend that stepped up and defended me. The rest just watched. I do not know if they were scared of him themselves or just did not care. He even came to my dad's house one day and beat me because I would not go back with him. My dad was at work, but my stepmom was there. She got a bat and told him that if he did not leave, she was going to hit him. He finally left. He was so bold to come into my dad's house and beat me. He did not care, but he knew my dad was not home.

When my dad came home, he went looking for him with his shotgun. He never found him. I never knew what he got out of beating me, but I guess it was about control. He punched me so hard, blackened my eyes, and busted my lip and then he'd get a hotel for a couple days. He definitely kept me away when he did that. Then his grandmother moved back to North Carolina to the home we were living in. It was her home; she was just letting him and me stay there. Even with her there, the abuse did not stop. He continued to hit me in front of her and when she would leave. She did not let us sleep together, so we had separate rooms after she came home.

He was so controlling that he locked me and his grandmother in the house from the outside so that I could not leave. His grandmother asked me to just leave him, but I could not. There were times he forced me to have sex with him after he beat me. I did not want to, but he made me. He cheated on me and did whatever he wanted to do. When I washed his clothes, I sometimes found condoms in his pockets. He denied everything. I came home one night and caught him in the bed with a woman. I was about six months pregnant at the time. He tried to fight me because I wanted to leave. There were times I left him when I got the chance but would go right back. When I tried to leave him, he'd take my son and would not let me take him with me. That was his way of making me stay or to keep me coming back. I took out warrants and everything but never went to court because I would let him talk me into coming back. When I left, he always sent me flowers or went and bought me the biggest diamond ring the jewelry store had, and I went right back to him. My stepmom and dad tried to shield me from him by changing the phone number, so he could not contact me when I went back home, but I still always gave him the new number.

He was a couple years older than me and sometimes showed up at my school looking through my classroom window with my son in his arms. He was always checking me and my clothes to see if I was cheating. I had a couple of friends that knew my situation, but they could not help me because they were going through the same thing.

One day, I got my hair braided, and we got into an argument, and he started hitting me. Then he reached for my hair and pulled several of my braids out. They came out from the root. My scalp was bleeding and bald. The sad part was that when he saw the damage he had done to my head, he kept on trying to pull more braids out. I was so tired of going through this, but I could not leave him completely alone. I left time after time, but I kept going back. I started to get really depressed and lost a lot of weight. Then I could not see any other way out. So, I took some of his grandmother's pills and tried to kill myself. He came home and saw me on the floor crying, and instead of taking me to the hospital, he took me to a hotel and forced me to drink some vinegar. I began to throw up. I started to feel like I did not care anymore.

My son was about three at the time. I left him again. He found me at a store in Rocky Mount and beat me inside the store and drug me by my hair outside and forced me inside the car. He hit me so hard that there was a gash in my forehead that was bleeding badly. Blood ran down my face. I cried, and people just watched. The people inside the store called the police, but by the time they got there, he had driven off with me inside the car. He took me into some woods and made me get out of the car. I was terrified. I knew he was going to kill me. A game warden drove up and saw him yelling and me crying, so he put me in his car and called my dad and told him he was taking me to the magistrate office to press charges.

The magistrate told me that they were not going to give me another warrant because I never showed up in court. Well, he went to the magistrate as well. He asked me to give him his rings and jewelry back, and I said no. The magistrate told me that I did not have to give him anything back if it was a gift. He told the magistrate that if I did not give him the jewelry back that he was going to cut my fingers off to get them back. He threatened me in front of the magistrate. After that, she gave me the warrant. Guess what? I still did not go to court. I went back to Maryland to stay with my mom for a while to get away from him.

After finding out that is where I was, he came to Maryland. He came to my mom's house. My brother was there, so we let him in thinking he would not try anything. He asked me if we could talk. So, we went into my mom's bedroom. She was at work at the time. He closed the door, and when I looked back, he was locking the door. Then he started trying to put his hands in my pants. He said he was trying to see if I had slept with anyone. I tried to push him off me, but then he began to choke me. I tried to scream, and I think my brother could hear the fumbling that was going on. My brother kicked the door open and jumped on him and told him that he better not ever hit me again. He left right after that.

My mom came home and was terribly upset. At this point, my mind was made up, and I knew I wanted out. I knew that if I did not get out, someone was going to get killed. I knew then that I had to protect my child and that my son needed his mom. I did not want my son to keep going through this back-and-forth cycle that I was in. I did not want him to keep seeing me crying and my face rearranged. I knew then that I did not love him anymore but had started to hate him. He did not really love me either, and I needed to get as far away from him as I could. My life depended on it. I went back to North Carolina without him knowing. He got into some trouble with the law that caused him to get a twelve-year sentence. That was my ticket out. I was so relieved that I did not have to worry about him beating me anymore. I was free. I did not have to worry about him harassing, beating, or controlling me ever again. I was able to come back to North Carolina and live without being scared he was going to find me.

I finally was able to move on with my life. I was able to have friends and enjoy my relationship with them. I was able to enjoy my family again. I moved back in with my dad and stepmom. Thank God, they let me come back home after all I had taken them through, the rebellion, the disobedience, and the disappointments. I was young, and I thought I was in love. I thought he loved me. I was at a place where I definitely needed to find myself because I had lost me.

Stephanie Mitchell

REFLECTIONS

I endured a physically abusive relationship. Have you ever been through an emotionally, physically, or verbally abusive relationship? Why did you not get out of it, or why did you finally get out of it?

_____
_____
_____
_____
_____
_____
_____
_____
_____
_____
_____
_____

Have you ever been through anything that caused you to lose yourself? What was it? What was your process of regaining your identity?

_____
_____
_____
_____
_____
_____
_____
_____
_____
_____
_____
_____

Chapter 4:

A Different Lifestyle

Even though I was still distracted, I went back to school to finish my senior year. I did not finish. I quit again. I still lived with my dad at the time. I finally got my GED. At the age of twenty, I got into a relationship with someone I had been dating. He did not have his own place, so I sometimes spent the night with him at his mom's house. I got pregnant with my second child. My other son was two years old. Living with my dad, stepmom, and siblings was crowded plus I was pregnant, so I needed my own space. Besides that, my dad was extremely strict and if you were not home when he locked the doors, you were not getting in the house. At least I thought he was strict, but as I became a mature adult, I realized that it was not being strict at all but just house rules. So, those nights that I hung out with my friends, I had to make sure I had somewhere to stay.

Given these circumstances, I decided to apply for low-income housing. The process did not take long. By the time my baby was three months old, my apartment was ready. Our new apartment had two bedrooms, and we moved in. I was so excited! It was time for me to acquire my own place even though I only had my bed and no other furniture. People gave me stuff for my place. When I could afford it, I furnished my whole place.

My son's father stayed with me most of the time. We hung out at the clubs from time to time with cousins and friends. Our relationship finally ended because he cheated. I found out he had another girlfriend for years, and we were both pregnant at the same time. Years later, partying and drinking got worse. I drank and smoked weed on the regular. There were always people at my place, and we partied all day long because at the time, I was not working. My income came from public assistance, and I braided hair   to make extra money to buy what I wanted and needed. When the kids were about five and seven, my neighbor kept them a lot while I was hanging out at the club. My neighbor and I were very close, and our kids were the same age, and I trusted her with them. Soon my apartment began to be the place where everybody hung out.

Finally, the time came when I was tired of sitting around doing nothing, and I decided to get a job. I started working at Black and Decker. They were only going to be open for four months, so I worked there until they closed. On the weekends, I still hung out. That job ended, but I loved making my own money, so I applied for another job that required me to work at night. My hours were 4 p.m. to midnight. I really liked this job because I was not really doing anything but standing for long periods of time.

I began dating a Jamaican guy that I met in the club. He was ten years older than me, but I liked him. He was so nice and treated me like a queen. Later, I found out he was a drug dealer, but I still stayed with him. I never saw him with drugs, and he never sold or had them in my presence. He had his own place, so I stayed with him sometimes. Even though I was in a relationship, I still wanted to hang out at the club every weekend with my friends. He was not okay with that, but I went anyway. We were very close and spent a lot of time together. He helped me with my bills and bought me anything I wanted. He really spoiled me. He was more of the settle down type, but I wanted to keep hanging out. I got drunk at the clubs and then called him to start arguments for no reason.

One day, I received a phone call from him saying he was arrested. He was set up and got picked up by the feds. He was locked up in the county jail for about a year. I went to visit him every weekend. The feds showed up at my door asking me questions about him. They knew I was his girlfriend, and they wanted to know if I had ever seen him with drugs or drug paraphernalia. Then they subpoenaed me to court when his court date came up. They came and picked me up. I was terrified. It turned out that I did not have to testify, so they took me back home. He ended up getting an eighteen-year sentence. I was so hurt, and I cried for days. I started drinking until I passed out. I continued to visit him until they transferred him to further out of state. Then we just talked on the phone.

I continued to drink and party. I sold marijuana but not for long because I was scared, especially with me living in public housing.

Years later, I still held it down with my job. Our hours changed to 5:30 p.m. till 4 a.m. I made good money on this job, so my mom came to stay with me to help me with the kids while I worked. I had fun on the weekends and still kept a lot of company. On Friday nights, I hung out and had to work Saturday mornings with hardly any sleep.

Some friends introduced me to a guy who had been hanging out at my apartment, and we got into a relationship. After several months, I became pregnant. I had not really thought about having any more kids, but it happened. I had a miscarriage, and I was hurt. I really wanted the baby. After the miscarriage, I got pregnant again, and we both were happy. It was his first child. Because of my pregnancy, I was not able to drink anymore but still kept a lot of company at my apartment. After about five months of being pregnant, we broke up because he started cheating and ended up getting someone else pregnant also.

A bout of depression set in, and I was incredibly angry with him about the cheating and the breakup. He left me for her, but I knew I had to get myself together for my baby and other sons.

After going one week past my due date, I had my third son. His dad was there at the hospital while I delivered. Everyone was excited and waited for my baby to come. I had an emergency C-section because my baby started going through fetal distress. My mom was in the delivery room with me. That was her first grandchild she got to see being born. I honestly thought he was not going to make it. I prayed because I was so scared about everything going on. The baby was fine. His father was there for him for whatever he needed.

I only had two bedrooms, so I knew I needed more room with three boys. I applied for Section 8 housing and got approved for a three-bedroom house for me and my boys. My mom was still with me to help out with the kids while I worked. I still worked the night shift and partied on the weekends. My rent went up because I was making good money. With the amount I was paying for rent, I could buy a home. So, that is what I did. I purchased my first brand new home at the age of thirty-two. I was so happy. I had a brand new three-bedroom and two full bath home that was just built. I was grateful for public housing and Section 8 helping me get ahead, but it was time for me to do better. I lived in the projects for eight years and in Section 8 housing for two years.

Even at my new home, I was still drinking and partying. I did not even know why, but I still did it. I think what made me slow up was my youngest son who was about seven at the time, finding me on my bathroom floor passed out. It scared him, and he thought I was dead. I knew then it was time to slow down or stop. I still drank from time to time but not as much as I did before. I felt God pulling on me. It was like He was telling me to get back in church. I shared that with my aunt, and she told me that it was God and that I needed to obey Him. I still did not go right away. I kept on living the way I was living, still going to the clubs with my friends, partying, and cooking out on the weekends.

By this time, my hours at my job changed to 6 p.m. to 6 a.m. I really loved my job and was going to keep hanging in there. The money was good, and I was able to put my house in order the way I wanted to. I worked in one room at a time. Even though I was working night hours, it was nothing for me to go out on the weekends and get up that morning and go to work. I even volunteered to work overtime to make extra money. I became one of the lead operators on my job because I was really good at making my production. They even had me train people that got hired. I received all kinds of incentives for outstanding work performance. Everything went well for me with my job. I just needed to get my life together.

After about three years of having my home, my job made an announcement that the company was closing down. I was so hurt. I had a mortgage. They did not close right then, but another company came in and brought them out. So, we were able to keep our jobs. I continued to work those long hours and provided for my family. I did really well with work and keeping up my home. I still knew and had it in my mind that I needed to get to church somewhere. I could still feel the pulling from God. I guess I did not want to give up my lifestyle. I enjoyed myself with my family and friends. We had cookouts and meetups every weekend. I still fraternized at clubs and bars drinking but not as much as I had.

At the time, I could not understand why I could not stop. Now, I know. One reason was the trauma I had gone through, and the other reason was that it was a generational curse of alcoholism. It was not until years later that I discovered the reasons why. I am just glad God never took His hands off of me. He kept me through it all, even all the times I could have gotten alcohol poisoning, started having problems with my liver, been pulled over, crashed, or killed someone was all God!

Stephanie Mitchell

REFLECTIONS

God kept me through all of my drinking, smoking weed, clubbing, and reckless behavior. What has God kept you through?

_____

_____

_____

_____

_____

_____

_____

_____

_____

_____

_____

Are you aligned with God's will for you? Do you feel Him tugging on your heart and spirit? Explain.

_____

_____

_____

_____

_____

_____

_____

_____

_____

_____

_____

Chapter 5:

Making a U-turn

After several years of enjoying my home, I was beyond grateful. My mom and kids were still with me. One day I met a guy at the store, and he asked me for my number. I did not know him personally but had seen him in the clubs, and we flirted with each other. After I gave him my number, we started talking. He came to my house, and we sat in the car and talked. He told me that he was married and asked me if I was okay with us being friends. I knew at that moment that I should end it, but I did not. We became closer and closer. He and his wife separated. He was like a best friend to me. We sat on my porch or met in the park to just drink, smoke weed, and talk. Then we entered into a relationship. Months later, he introduced me to his family. My family met him as well. We were together all the time when we were not working. We spent the whole day together, and when he got home, we talked on the phone until one of us fell asleep.

I still felt that pulling and tugging from God. So, finally I started visiting church. He went with me a few times, but he told me that he was not ready for church and did not expect him to go. So, I went alone. My girlfriend went with me sometimes. One day while sitting in church, I felt the Lord prompting me to get up and walk to the front during the altar call. That day I rededicated my life to Christ. I grew up in church but stopped going when I was a teenager. Not only did I join the church, but I also got baptized again. I wanted to be baptized again because I wanted to be totally connected to God. Before I went down in the water, I prayed and asked God to let me come out of that water different.

I wanted to be new. I wanted my life to be changed forever. I believe He did just that. My relationship with my boyfriend changed. Our relationship was based on smoking, drinking, and sex. After that, I could not let him touch me anymore. God took the taste of alcohol and weed away. I stopped drinking and smoking. I stopped hanging out at the clubs also. When I would not have sex with him, he got upset and left. I did not know how to explain to him what I was going through. He could never understand it. Our relationship began to fade away. He started talking to other women while we were still together. So, I finally ended our relationship. He moved on. I was okay for about a month then I started missing him so much. I could not get him out of my mind. About two months later, I reached out to him to say happy birthday. He did not answer, so I left a message on his voicemail. I still thought about him a lot. I considered taking him back. Then God showed me in a dream that he had a woman pregnant. That was confirmed through a friend of mine when he told me he saw him with a woman, and she was pregnant. So, I moved on.

I had now come to a place in my life where I was tired of dating, tired of men and did not want anybody. I did not date anyone for three years. I did not even talk to any guys on the phone. I just focused on my relationship with God. I became very intimate with God. I had lots of dreams that seemed so real. I even heard His voice. Some of the people I spent time with started to fade away. We separated. I was no longer doing the things we used to do, so people stopped inviting me to a lot of events. I was okay with that. I did not desire to be around a lot of stuff anymore.

I kept pursuing God, getting to know Him and the things of God. My prayer partner came to my house one day to get her hair braided. My back was bothering me that day. After I finished, she asked me to come into my kitchen, so she could pray for my mom. After she prayed for my mom, she reached over me and started praying over my back. A presence came upon me like I had never experienced before. My hands went up in the air without my control, and I began to cry and praise God. My mouth was moving but nothing was coming out. This went on for several minutes. She told me that it was my tongues. I was just baptized with the Holy Ghost and fire. I cannot even describe the feeling. I know in the end there was a calmness, like I was not myself. It was the best feeling. Then I began feeling like I wanted more of God, not just going to church, listening to the choir and the sermon but more. I was at a place where I knew there had to be more to God than I knew at that time.

Church continued to be my Sunday activity, but I still felt like there was something else needed. My desire became to see things happen in the supernatural. I wanted to see God move. The church I was a member of at the time was a Bible teaching church focusing on that. You saw people getting saved but not delivered or set free. You did not see a lot of laying on of the hands. That is when I got revelation from God that it was time to transition to a five-fold ministry. That was what He was calling me to.

God placed that hunger for more on the inside of me. I was at that church for eight years and had grown quite a bit. But God called me to an apostolic ministry. So, I visited other places. My coworkers told me about a five-fold ministry in my town, so I visited there. The first time I visited, I loved the way they worshipped God. Everything I sought was there. People worshipped, shouted, got breakthroughs, and got healed and delivered. The worship was outstanding. The members flowed however the Holy Spirit led. Sometimes, the glory was so tangible, the pastor did not get to preach. I loved that corporate worship, and everyone was of one accord. No one was looking around, but everyone was getting what they needed.

I visited that church for about eight or nine months before joining. Everyone was so friendly, but I had walls up because of so much hurt that I had been through. I went to church and after service, I left and did not socialize. I did not know a lot of people and really did not want to get close with anyone at that time. I was not interested in making new friends or socializing with anyone. Some ladies came up to me after service and started talking. Eventually I started socializing more and made friends with some of the women.

As time passed, I began serving on the usher board. That was unusual for me because I was never a people person. I definitely did not smile a lot. They needed help, so I joined to help. After ushering for a while and some trips to the altar, God began to do something in me. Those walls began to come down. I smiled more, and I was able to embrace people. I really began to love people. I started loving people like never before. I did not feel withdrawn from people the way I once did. I was able to socialize more and embrace what He was doing in me. I made real relationships and friendships with some of the ladies at church. We became remarkably close. I just had to let go of past friendships that were disappointing and be open to receive new friendships.

REFLECTIONS

I got a taste of who God really is and longed for more. Are you seeking more of God? How?

_____
_____
_____
_____
_____
_____
_____
_____
_____
_____
_____

Are you allowing God to tear down walls in every area of your life, so it can be all He wants it to be? How does that feel?

_____
_____
_____
_____
_____
_____
_____
_____
_____
_____
_____
_____

Have you been baptized with the Holy Ghost and fire? Do you desire it? Explain.

_____
_____

_____
_____
_____
_____
_____
_____
_____
_____
_____
_____
_____

Chapter 6:
The Day My Life Changed Forever

"He healeth the broken in heart and bindeth up their wounds" (Psalm 147:3, KJV).

Looking back over my life and reflecting on all the things I have overcome; I give all the thanks to my Lord and Savior because without Him I could not have made it. I am grateful that He was with me every step of the way, even when I was not aware of it. I used to think that when we go through tragedies and trials, we must have done something wrong. The more I drew closer to God and got to know Him, the more I understood. A lot of times, we blame things on the devil. Some things are the devil, and some things God allows us to go through, not to punish us but to draw us closer to Him.

Have you ever had your heart broken? My heart was broken, crushed, torn into pieces, or however you want to say it. I had a thorn in my side and experienced a tragedy I did not even think I could recover from. But to God be all the glory. He was my healer, comforter, restorer, protector, strong tower, mind regulator, and my strength. My God was there to help me through it all.

On January 18,1991, I gave birth to my first son. He was a healthy eight-pound boy. I named him Anthony Tremaine Walker. He was my bundle of joy. He was the first grandchild in our family. At first, I did not see having a baby as a blessing because I was eighteen years old and still in school. In the end, he was indeed a blessing. I was a single parent after his dad and I split, raising a child alone. I did my best to make sure he was taken care of and had everything he needed. He was full of energy and very advanced. He started walking at nine months and was talking very clearly. He was very spoiled, and everyone loved him. I thank God that He made a way for me to nurture, care for, and love my child the I way I should have.

I watched him grow into a young man. He loved playing basketball and played for his high school. He also joined ROTC while in high school. He was not perfect but loved his family. Then he had children of his own. I admired the relationship he had with his children and knew he loved them dearly. You almost never saw him without his kids.

On March 13, 2015, my life changed forever. That is a day I will never forget. That morning, I got up and went to work like any normal day. Nothing seemed strange or different that morning. Around 11a.m., I received a phone call from a close friend stating that my son's truck was at the park, and there was crime scene tape all around it. She said she really did not know what happened and that the police had the area blocked off. When I got off the phone with her, I screamed and yelled like never before, not knowing what happened but just because I knew whatever it was, my son was involved. At that moment, I went into some kind of shock. I felt deep down inside that something had happened to him. I scared my coworkers, and they came running to see what was wrong. They asked me over and over what happened, but I could not even talk.

One of my coworkers prayed for me. Our supervisor was not there at the time, but they called her, and she told them to take me home. When I arrived home, my mom was on the phone with the doctor at the emergency room. My son's children were there at the time. They were two and four then. My mom gave me the phone. The doctor told me who he was and that my son was there, and he had been shot in the head. I dropped the phone and began to scream. I knew that because he was shot in the head his chances of survival were limited. The kids were looking, and they did not understand what was happening. I tried to get myself together.

My supervisor came and drove me to the hospital. On the way there, I prayed that God would let him live and that he would one day be able to tell his testimony. When I got there, they took me into one of those counseling rooms. I knew then that my son was gone. When I entered the room, my son's girlfriend, her mother, my stepsister, and some friends were already in there crying. The doctor came in and confirmed what I had feared. My son was dead. He did not survive his injuries. I wept and wept. I asked the doctor if I could see him. At that moment, I was in denial and had to be sure that it was him.

They took me to the back where they had been trying to revive him. There he was, my baby, my first-born child, lying there lifeless on that table. He was twenty-four years old at the time. I wanted to grab him and hold him one last time. They said I could not touch him because it was a crime scene now. Someone took my son's life, and I could not contaminate the evidence. I just cried and cried. I felt like a piece of my heart had been ripped from my chest. I felt sad, mad, helpless, and hurt. I wanted someone to tell me that it was all a dream. I wanted to wake up, and he would still be alive.

The doctor said that there was no way that he could have survived his injuries. Not only was he shot in the head, but he was also shot in three other places. The doctor said the shot to the head was the one that killed him. The young man that shot him left him for dead. I will never forget that moment of seeing him lying on that table. I thought about him lying there and wondered what his last words were. I had to leave the hospital knowing that I would never see my son again. He was murdered by one of his old acquaintances. The district attorney told me that he was murdered because of a girl. The young man that took his life thought he was trying to talk to his girlfriend.

I went home and lay across my bed. I did not want to see anyone. I just wanted to be alone. My family and friends came right over. My son visited me on Monday. He passed that Friday. If I had known it would be the last time I would see him, I would have

Stephanie Mitchell

hugged him and kissed him. I would have told him how much I love him. But we never know when it will be our last time seeing our loved ones. The grieving process was extremely hard for me. I isolated myself for about two days. I stayed in my room and would not eat.

My family and friends came and laid on my bed and cried with me. They comforted me and prayed with me. I thank God for the support that I had from family and friends during that time. We were also blessed by neighbors and people that we did not know. I was not able to do his arrangements alone because I could not focus mentally. I also had help from his father's family with the arrangements. There were so many people coming and showing support. I became overwhelmed by so much company. I knew their intentions were good, but I wanted to be alone. I knew that being alone was not good, so I continued to socialize.

The young man that took his life was hiding out. The detective assigned to my son's case was very good. He did a good job communicating with me. He told me that they weren't going to stop looking for him. The day of my son's funeral, he came to my house and told me they had found him, and he had been arrested. The detective asked me if he could hug me. He was so sympathetic. I felt relieved that my son's murderer had been caught.

After the funeral, I went back to work that next week which was too soon. I thought maybe if I did, it would keep my mind off it. I worked a full-time job and a part-time job. I eventually quit my part-time job. I had moments where I was easily agitated, could not focus on my job, and made mistakes. I also had breakdowns while at work. I still attended church as usual but still felt empty.

I tried to be strong but was hurting. I prayed to God and asked Him to help me through this tragedy. I continued to talk with Him and read scriptures dealing with grief and pain. God started to work on me from the inside out. He began to heal my broken heart.

I thank Him for keeping my mind during this time. I thank Him for giving me a forgiving heart. I know my relationship with Him makes all the difference. I never was upset with God, but I did not understand why He let it happen. I did not stop pursuing God but drew closer to Him. I told God that I trust Him.

Even though my son is no longer here physically, he lives in my heart, through his children and the memories we shared. I still think about him and will always remember him. I will always treasure the good memories. I used to go to his grave all the time to sit, think, and cry. I wish he was still here. Now that God has given me peace, I go there only to put new flowers on his grave.

To me, he is no longer there but in my heart. He is always with me, so I do not need to go to his grave to feel close to him.

Months later, the young man that took his life had a bond hearing and was denied bond. Then he took a plea deal that was twenty-four to forty-eight years. The DA asked me if I was okay with it. I said yes. I did not want to have to sit in the courtroom and listen to how he killed my son. No amount of time he got was going to bring my son back. I also believe in forgiveness. I had to, not for him but for me.

None of our suffering is without purpose. Second Corinthians 4:8-9 says, "We are afflicted in every way, but not crushed; perplexed, but not driven to despair; persecuted, but not forsaken; struck down, but not destroyed." Also, Second Corinthians 1:3-4 says, "Blessed be the God and Father of our Lord Jesus Christ, the Father of mercies and God of all comfort, who comforts us in all our affliction, so that we may be able to comfort those who are in an affliction, with the comfort with which we ourselves are comforted by God."

Suffering equips some of us for ministry. Suffering prepares us for more glory. God wants us to look to Him when we are suffering. I encourage you today, if you are going through a loss and are grieving, just know that God will give you the comfort and strength you need to get through it. He will give you peace in your situation. That peace will help you to move on. Yes, you will miss your loved ones. And yes, you will still think about them. But that peace keeps you from becoming stagnant. It is okay to seek counseling if you need to. Do whatever helps. What you do not want is for grief to become a stronghold. It may help to talk to someone.

Grief is a process, and healing will not happen suddenly. The worst thing you can do is isolate yourself. Isolation makes it more difficult to heal and gives the enemy room to play with your thoughts and can bring depression. Reach out to people to talk about your feelings. A good support group or support network will help. You can also journal your feelings to help with the healing process.

REFLECTIONS

Have you experienced God as a Comforter? How?

_____

_____

_____

_____

_____

_____

_____

_____

_____

_____

Are there people you have had to forgive for your own peace?
Who and when?

_____

_____

_____

_____

_____

_____

_____

_____

_____

_____

How have you comforted others in the way that God comforted
you?

_____

_____

_____

_____
_____
_____
_____
_____
_____
_____
_____
_____
_____

Chapter 7:
Loss of My Mom

"The Lord is near to the brokenhearted and saves the crushed in spirit" (Psalm 34: 18, ESV).

My mom and I had an unbreakable relationship. She lived with me for many years. She was my best friend, and I could talk to her about anything. She was a very straightforward tell-you-like-it-is kind of person. Everyone knew she was that way. She had a sweet spirit, but she would put you in your place if she needed to. She never sugarcoated anything. She was a loving person and loved to cook. She found her peace in the kitchen and loved cooking for her family and getting her family together. Everyone loved my mom's cooking. She cooked most of the food for our holidays or family dinners. Her mac and cheese brought her notoriety. She also was the one who kept everyone's kids while we worked or if we had something to do.

Back in 2012, she was diagnosed with cirrhosis of the liver, so she decided to make some lifestyle changes. Upon making those changes, her health started to decline. She got extremely sick. The doctors said that she would not live a year. They told us to prepare for her funeral arrangements and to call the hospice. That day I was so hurt, and the doctor did not have any sympathy when he said that. I did not want to lose her. My family and I began to pray. We had everyone praying for her. I met with my siblings to tell them what the doctor said, and we prayed and believed that God had the final say.

Her cousins came to our home and prayed for her. On some Sundays when she went to church, she got in the prayer line. She believed God for her healing. She went back and forth to the doctor every two weeks for a while to have fluid pulled from her liver. Then she went an entire year without the fluid coming back. That was a miracle. She was feeling great. After about a year and a half, the fluid came back, and she had to go to the doctor every two weeks again. My brother and sister-in-law took her to her appointments.

She still was able to cook, clean, and drive like she normally would. Actually, she was able to do whatever she wanted. She lived a normal life even after the doctors gave up on her. Then the doctors told her that her kidneys were going into failure and that she would need dialysis. She started dialysis in February 2020 and went for five months; she hated it. She was very weak afterwards and said that it was no way anyone should have to live. Although she was weak after dialysis, she still was able to live a normal life for a while. Her blood pressure kept dropping, and they did not know why. She was back and forth in the hospital at this point.

Covid was raging then, so no one could be there with her. The last time she went to the hospital, she felt so bad she could not walk and was disoriented. We had to call the EMS for her. She was in the hospital in Roanoke Rapids. We were able to visit her but only one at a time. We had to take turns going to sit with her. She was there for about a month. After running tests, they discovered that my mom had sepsis and began treating her with antibiotics. On July 27, 2020, I was about to do a photoshoot for my birthday which was July 29. That day we got the call that my mom was unresponsive and was put on life support.

My siblings and I went to the hospital, and I do not know if she knew we were there. She coded while we were there, and they brought her back. The doctor told us that it would not be long. I stayed by her side and held her hand until her heart took its last beat. My mom passed away that day from sepsis. Sepsis is a potentially life-threatening condition that occurs when the body's response to an infection damages its own tissues.

Sepsis may progress to septic shock. This is a dramatic drop in the blood pressure that can lead to severe organ problems and death. If sepsis is caught in time, it can be treated. For her, it was already in her bloodstream, and it spread too quickly. They asked me to step out until they cleaned her up, so I went in the waiting room. I cried and cried. My siblings were gone, so I was there by myself. When they came back to get me after they cleaned her up, I could not go back in there. They asked me if I was sure and said that she looked like she was just sleeping, but I could not.

I left the hospital and went home knowing my mom was not going to be there anymore. I called my aunt, my mom's sister, to tell her she had transitioned. Driving home from the hospital, I was so hurt. I felt like a piece of my heart was ripped out. I was numb. Family and friends visited and brought food, water, drinks, and things like that. They came every day. Even my neighbors were coming over bringing stuff. Everyone loved my mom. She was a lovable person.

My mom did a pre-burial where she had already picked out and paid for most of her funeral stuff. I just had to plan where to have the funeral and do her obituary. My aunt helped me with that. She was a member of a local church, so we had her funeral there. The day we went to view her body for the first time, which was right before her viewing, I was terribly upset and disappointed because she did not look like herself. I told the funeral home that I was not pleased. They told me it was because she had been sick. She was very dark. They told me that they would lighten her up. The Holy Spirit spoke to me and said, "It's just her body." Then there was a sense of peace.

During the funeral, I thought I was going to hold it together, but I did not. I broke down when they played particular songs. I hurt so badly. I was angry, hurt, and disappointed. I was angry with her for leaving and angry with God because I expected to see her healed. So, I wrestled with that. I asked God to extend her life like He did for Hezekiah in the Bible. God reminded me that He

Stephanie Mitchell

had given her eight extra years to be with us back in 2012 when the doctors said she would not live a year. I had to be honest with God and tell Him how I felt.

It took me a long time to realize that I was angry with God. I repented and asked Him to forgive me. Later I realized it was selfish of me to want her to stay knowing she was suffering. Going through that process was not easy. We had her funeral on a Tuesday and could not bury her until Thursday because of the weather. After her burial, I went out to eat with one of my lady friends and then went home, packed my bags, and went to Myrtle Beach by myself. I needed to get away and needed to be alone. Company was around for two weeks during the process of her death. I needed to get away. While I was there, I was able to cry like I wanted to and talk to God. I got some groceries for the weekend, and I did not leave my room until I got ready to leave. I checked into the hotel on Thursday, and Friday night, my throat started feeling funny. That Saturday morning, I got ready to head back home, and I was not feeling well. I had a runny nose and was sneezing. I had to stop and get something to take because I had also started having chills. I thought I was coming down with a cold.

Covid was bad at that time so when I got home, I quarantined. On Sunday, I got tested but had to wait until Wednesday to get my results. My results came back positive for Covid. So, not only was I grieving, but I was also sick with Covid. I started crying and felt bad because I had just lost my mom and had to be shut up in my bedroom for two weeks without any contact from anyone. People were dying left and right from Covid, and I was really scared. I was scared I was going to die. I questioned God and asked Him why, why was I sick at a time like this when I had just lost my mom.

I questioned why I was the only one that got sick out of all the people I was around. Nobody else in my house was sick. Not that I wanted anyone else to be sick, but I wondered why me. God reminded me that I should be grateful that I was not lying in the hospital on a ventilator. My case was not bad at all. I hurt badly, lost my taste and smell, and had cold symptoms, but I was still blessed.

Weeks later, I could not even sit in my living room or eat at my kitchen table. My mom and I sat at the kitchen table every day and talked. I could not go into my mom's room either. I kept her door closed. It was hard living in my house without her. Honestly, I was ready to sell my house and relocate. I attempted to go into her room, and I looked down and saw her shoes. I almost ran out of there. I got so emotional. Eventually, I went to grief counseling. It really helped. There are five stages of grief. They are denial, anger, bargaining, depression, and acceptance. Understanding the grief process can help you with acceptance and healing. She had me deal with the hurt. I had to eat at my kitchen table and go into my mom's room and pray for a couple minutes some days. After about a month of counseling, I was able to clean out her stuff in my dining room, like her mail, medications, etc. Then I was eventually able to sit in my living room again.

Do I still have moments? Yes. I deal with them. I cry, I talk about how I feel with a close friend, or I talk to God. I prayed and asked God to heal my broken heart. I asked Him to comfort and strengthen me, and He did. Healing is a process, but we are responsible for our healing. We cannot run, hide, or keep busy, so we do not have to deal with it. I mean you can, but it makes the process longer. It is better to sit and deal with the hurt. It's difficult to deal with the hurt, but we must let God do the mending, the healing, the strengthening, and comforting.

There are so many stages of grief, and I am at the stage of acceptance. I encourage anyone who is grieving from the loss of a loved one to seek grief counseling. A healthy community of people who support you during a time of grief also helps. It is also important to talk with someone about your feelings because it's best to let them out. Cry, grieve, talk, and heal. Just do not let your grief become a stronghold. Matthew 5:4 says, "Blessed

Stephanie Mitchell

are those who mourn, for they will be comforted." And the good thing is that we are not alone in the grieving process and can be assured that we will make it through it because Isaiah 53:4 says, "Surely he has borne our griefs and carried our sorrows; yet we esteemed him stricken, smitten by God, and afflicted." Jesus Christ already bore our griefs on the cross, and we will get to the other side of sorrow.

REFLECTIONS

When my mother died, I did not think I would make it. Have you experienced a situation you did not think you would make it through? What was it and how did you overcome it?

_____

_____

_____

_____

_____

_____

_____

_____

_____

_____

_____

What does Isaiah 53:4 mean to you personally?

_____

_____

_____

_____

_____

_____

_____

_____

_____

_____

_____

How do you deal with grief? Do you isolate yourself or need the presence of family around? Explain.

_____

_____

_____
_____
_____
_____
_____
_____
_____
_____
_____
_____
_____
_____

Chapter 8:

Release and Be Free

I have been through a journey of hurt, pain, disappointment, rejection, physical abuse, and sexual abuse. After years, I was able to see and understand why I did some of the things I did and why I reacted the way I did. Going back and revisiting the little girl who went through all those things was not easy but necessary in order to heal. A lot of our trauma or pain started in our childhood. For so many years, I suppressed all that hurt and pain. I became numb to it. I never talked to anyone about what I went through as a child. I pushed it back into the back of my mind like it never happened to the point that I almost forgot about it. Nobody wants to be reminded of those painful experiences. We just want to forget about them.

When you have been molested as a child, it can open doors to perversion. I discovered this later when I was grown. I grew up thinking it was okay to sleep with multiple people. The more I grew in Christ, the more He revealed a lot of truth to me, especially the whys. I was able to understand why I struggled with fear and rejection, why I was always defensive if I felt like someone was trying to control me, and why I disconnected from people because of rejection. I understood why I always felt like I did not fit in in some places, why I was uncomfortable being alone and going places alone, and why I was always seeking attention from men. Also, I understood why I could not keep a relationship and could not communicate. I was always shutting down. One minute I wanted a relationship, and one minute I did not. Then I broke off the relationship.

I could not understand why I could sleep with men that I did not love at all. Honestly, I could not love men the right way. I did not hate men but could not love them either. I thought I did, but I did not. I just enjoyed having sex with them. A part of me was scared to let someone have my heart. Then the Lord later revealed to me that sex had become a coping mechanism for me. I depended on sex to get that feeling of what I thought was love and comfort. Just being in a man's arms was security for me. I looked for love in the wrong places. Looking for someone to love, comfort, protect, and make me feel good was what I was doing without realizing it. There were men that I hurt because of it. Being in a relationship and sleeping with men was misleading when I did not love them. I loved God, but when I lost my son, I still fell back into needing a man to comfort me.

I prayed and asked God to comfort me and told Him that He was my comforter but still looked for comfort elsewhere. I was longing for immediate comfort and trying to take away the pain that I was feeling. That is when God showed me the coping mechanism.

After God revealed my brokenness to me, I decided to start the healing process. Many of us can walk around dressed up on the outside but broken on the inside. That was me for many years. I had to be honest with myself and admit that I was broken. I started praying to God to heal my broken heart from every hurt, pain, anger, rage, perversion, unforgiveness, father wounds, mother wounds, rejection, jealousy, lust, gossip, and slander. All these things were from a broken heart.

I continuously asked God to remove those things from my heart. I had to allow Him to get to the root of my pain. You cannot just deal with the surface, but you have to deal with the root. I got in prayer lines at church every opportunity and went to the altar repeatedly. I was determined to be healed. I also decided to go through inner healing and deliverance.

There were layers of damage, so I went through it several times. I also went through grief counseling twice, when my son passed and when my mom passed. Healing also took me partnering with the Holy Spirit in prayer and believing every word that God says about me. Then I had to allow Him to renew my mind, releasing me and talking to Him about how I felt and allowing Him to have His way in me and through me.

I always asked for a heart after His own. Spending time with Him and in His word helped me to know Him, knowing He is my provider, my protector, my keeper, my healer, my restorer, my comforter, my strength, and my security. I do not have to look for those things in a man. When people ask me how I got over losing my son, I tell them that it was all God. My relationship with Him made all the difference. Without Him, I could not have made it. I am so grateful for God keeping my mind through it all, the healing, the depression, the abuse, the suicide attempt, the alcohol, the drugs, the disappointments, and hurt. It was all Him. All the glory belongs to Him.

I am not perfect, and I am still a work in progress. God has me in a place now where I am discovering who I am. I am enjoying learning about me. I am enjoying spending time with myself, and it feels great. I have learned to love me. That was one of the reasons I could not love anyone else the right way. I did not love myself. I had to forgive myself for my past mistakes and failures along with the people that had hurt, abused, mistreated, and disappointed me. It can be hard to forgive, but we have to ask God to help us.

Forgiveness is not for the person we are forgiving but for us. So, we can be free.

Unforgiveness can have us bound and block so many things God wants to do in our lives. God had me in a season of pruning and growing. Pruning is a process done for healthy growth. John 15:1-2 says, "I am the true vine, and my father is the vinedresser. Every branch in me that does not bear fruit he takes away, and every branch that does bear fruit he prunes." There were some things that He wanted to prune out of me. There were also some areas in my life that needed growth. In order to bear fruit and walk in the purpose God has for me, I had to be pruned. He prunes us for our good so that we can be spiritually healthy and

Stephanie Mitchell

fruitful. He had to prune the things I wanted to hold on to that were unhealthy for me.

I had a habit of holding on to people or places that God wanted me to let go of. He revealed to me that He was making room for the new. He also revealed people's true motives and intentions toward me, so I could take necessary steps to cut ties with people. He also had to renew my mind from some negative thinking. Everything that I had been through had shaped my thinking. I was always thinking everywhere I went people would reject me, or everyone that came into my life would leave. He also was teaching me the root of issues and how to walk-in freedom.

During this process, I am also learning how to be patient with people, learning how to listen and be slow to speak, and how to keep my mouth closed when I need to. I had to learn to not compare my process to others because I did not understand why I went through what I went through. God really showed me myself during that season. If I asked Him what was wrong with someone else when I was offended, He would show me what was wrong with me. That was the time for me to repent and release what was in my heart. It helped me understand that sometimes we have to examine ourselves. We have to ask God to search our hearts. It was a part of my growth process. But I am so grateful for that season God had me in. It was necessary for my spiritual growth.

As I said before, I am a work in progress. I would encourage you to seek healing from any trauma or pain. He is our healer. Sit with Him. Release the people who hurt you. Forgive them so that you too can be free. Allow God to renew your mind. We have to change our thinking and learn to cast down those thoughts that are unhealthy. Second Corinthians 10:5 says, "Casting down imaginations, and every high thing that exalts itself against the knowledge of God and bringing into captivity every thought to the obedience of Christ."

Talk to someone you can trust about how you feel. I recommend counseling. It really helped me. Read your word regularly and pray often, which protects you and equips you against any attacks. Let God become your focus, your motivation, and your hope during tough times. Romans 5:3-4 tells us "Not only so, but we also glory in our sufferings, because we know that suffering produces perseverance; character; and character, hope."

Suffering has a purpose. James 1:2-4 says, "Consider it pure joy, my brothers, and sisters, whenever you face trials of many kinds, because you know that the testing of your faith produces perseverance. Let perseverance finish its work so that you may be mature and complete, not lacking anything."

You might be tempted to do things your way, but you should surrender and allow God to do the mending!

REFLECTIONS

Have you overcome any suppressed childhood traumas or pain? How?

_____
_____
_____
_____
_____
_____
_____
_____
_____
_____
_____
_____
_____

Has God revealed any of the roots of problems you experienced as a child or an adult? What did He show you?

_____
_____
_____
_____
_____
_____
_____
_____
_____
_____
_____
_____
_____

Does God have you in a season of pruning? What does it look like?

_____

_____
_____
_____
_____
_____
_____
_____
_____
_____
_____
_____
_____

What is the overall message this book relays to you?

_____
_____
_____
_____
_____
_____
_____
_____
_____
_____
_____
_____
_____

About the Author

Stephanie Mitchell is a resident of Rocky Mount NC and has resided there since the age of sixteen. She is the mother of two sons, Antonio Morgan and Markeith Mitchell. Her three grandchildren hold a special place in her heart.

As Stephanie started writing *Healing Past the Hurt*, she continued to work as a state board-certified cosmetologist, which has been her occupation for the last ten years. She is the proprietor of Braids and Styles by Stephanie LLC. Hairstyling has been a longtime passion for her. Her salon is located in downtown Rocky Mount.

Stephanie is also the founder of Mending Our Hearts, a support group for women who have lost children. She has a passion and heart to see others overcome trauma. It is her desire to aid those in need of healing as a coach and through facilitating group workshops.

Contact Stephanie at authorstephanie2023@gmail.com.

CPSIA information can be obtained
at www.ICGtesting.com
Printed in the USA
LVHW052052290423
745638LV00007B/64